W9-CLD-419

Reading
Shakespeare
Today

The
MERCHANT
of VENICE

Caitlyn Paley

Cavendish
Square

New York

Published in 2016 by Cavendish Square Publishing, LLC
243 5th Avenue, Suite 136, New York, NY 10016

Copyright © 2016 by Cavendish Square Publishing, LLC

First Edition

No part of this publication may be reproduced, stored in a retrieval system, or transmitted in any form or by any means—electronic, mechanical, photocopying, recording, or otherwise—without the prior permission of the copyright owner. Request for permission should be addressed to Permissions, Cavendish Square Publishing, 243 5th Avenue, Suite 136, New York, NY 10016. Tel (877) 980-4450; fax (877) 980-4454.

Website: cavendishsq.com

This publication represents the opinions and views of the author based on his or her personal experience, knowledge, and research. The information in this book serves as a general guide only. The author and publisher have used their best efforts in preparing this book and disclaim liability rising directly or indirectly from the use and application of this book.

CPSIA Compliance Information: Batch #CW16CSQ

All websites were available and accurate when this book was sent to press.

Cataloging-in-Publication Data

Paley, Caitlyn.
Merchant of Venice / by Caitlyn Paley.
p. cm. — (Reading Shakespeare today)
Includes index.
ISBN 978-1-5026-1045-4 (hardcover) ISBN 978-1-5026-1046-1 (e-book)
1. Shakespeare, William, 1564-1616. Merchant of Venice — Juvenile literature. I. Paley, Caitlyn. II. Title.
PR2825.P35 2016
822.3'3—d23

Editorial Director: David McNamara
Editor: Andrew Coddington
Copy Editor: Rebecca Rohan
Art Director: Jeffrey Talbot
Designer: Stephanie Flecha
Senior Production Manager: Jennifer Ryder-Talbot
Production Editor: Renni Johnson
Photo Research: J8 Media

The photographs in this book are used by permission and through the courtesy of:
Quim Llenas/Cover/Getty Images, cover; Shutterstock, front and back covers and through out the book; David Stanley from Nanaimo, Canada (Shakespeare`s Globe Theatre Uploaded by russavia) [CC BY 2.0 (http://creativecommons.org/licenses/by/2.0), via Wikimedia Commons, 5; Sarah L. Voisin/The Washington Post/Getty Images, 9; 18, 20, 45, 53, 57; Buena Vista/Getty Images, 13; SONY PICTURES/ Steve Braun/Album/Superstock, 14; Antonio Canal (called Canaletto) (Italy, Venice, 1697-1768) Public domain/via Wikimedia Commons, 17; Universal History Archive/Getty Images, 22; Jane Hobson/Rex Features/AP Images, 27; Sir James Dromgole Linton/Private Collection/Bridgeman Images, 30; The Washington Post/Getty Images, 34, 55; Culture Club/Getty Images, 39; Bettina Strenske/Photoshot/Newscom, 58; Georges De Keerle/Getty Images, 61; Agnostic Preachers Kid at en.wikipedia [CC BY-SA 3.0 (http://creativecommons.org/licenses/by-sa/3.0) or GFDL (http://www.gnu.org/copyleft/fdl.html), from Wikimedia Commons, 67; Richard Westall [CC BY-SA 4.0 (http://creativecommons.org/licenses/by-sa/4.0), via Wikimedia Commons 72; Christie's Images/Superstock, 78; Haywood Magee/Picture Post/Getty Images, 80; Henry Wallis/ Private Collection/Look and Learn/Illustrated Papers Collection/Bridgeman Images, 81; Joe Steele/The Scotsman/Zuma Press, 83; William Shakespeare Public domain, via Wikimedia Commons, 85; Universal History Archive/UIG via Getty images, 87; Andrew Brown/Private Collection/Look and Learn/Illustrated Papers Collection/Bridgeman Images, 88; English School/Private Collection/Look and Learn/Bridgeman Images, 91.

Printed in the United States of America

CONTENTS

Introduction

Shakespeare and His World

The work of William Shakspeare is everywhere. His story lines pop up in movies, television shows, and books. Hundreds of his quotations make their way into everyday conversation. Shakespeare's continued popularity is staggering, considering that he died around four hundred years ago. Many literary critics cite Shakespeare as the most influential writer of all time. Others wonder if he could have possibly written all 38 plays and 154 sonnets credited to him. Indeed, there is a lot of uncertainty about William Shakespeare and his life. So who was the man behind remarkable plays like *The Merchant of Venice*, *Romeo and Juliet*, and *Macbeth*?

On April 23, 1564, William Shakespeare was born in Stratford-upon-Avon, a town in England's countryside. Records reveal little about Shakespeare's childhood. Some scholars speculate that Shakespeare never attended school but rather taught himself to read. In fact, not much is known about Shakespeare until he turned eighteen. At the age of eighteen, Shakespeare married a twenty-six-year-old woman named Anne Hathaway. Anne was already pregnant with their first child, a daughter they named Susanna.

Shakespeare's theater company performed at the Globe Theatre in London.

Shakespeare's family grew quickly. Anne delivered twins Hamnet and Judith in 1584. Hamnet's death at the age of eleven was most likely the biggest personal tragedy in Shakespeare's life.

Shakespeare moved to London to pursue a career as an actor and playwright in 1585. He worked for the preeminent theater company of the era, the Lord Chamberlain's Men. Yet, surprisingly, Shakespeare first achieved fame with the publication of two poems. *Venus and Adonis* first appeared in 1583, followed by the *Rape of Lucrece* shortly thereafter. These two poems helped establish Shakespeare as a respected poet. And while Shakespeare would go on to publish 154 sonnets, today we regard him first and foremost as a playwright.

Like Shakespeare's poems, his plays were immensely successful in his day. Shakespeare quickly rose through the ranks with his theater company, becoming a partner in The Lord Chamberlain's Men. The company performed at the Globe Theater in London. Going to the theater in Shakespeare's day was a vastly different experience than it is for today's theatergoers. In the sixteenth century, plays were entertainment for the masses. Shakespeare's works are comedies, tragedies, and historical plays, but all aim to appeal to both highbrow and lowbrow audiences. Sophisticated wordplay is intermixed with crass and bawdy jokes. In a Shakespeare play, there really is something for everyone.

William Shakespeare died on his birthday, April 23, at the age of fifty-two. He had achieved wealth and fame through his writing in his lifetime. Yet he never could have predicted that his plays would take on a life of their own. Shakespeare's writing continues to influence famous writers today. His canon has shaped not just the stories we tell, but also society's approach to larger philosophical issues. Nowhere is this more apparent than with a play like *The Merchant of Venice*, which asks its readers to consider the assumptions we make based on appearances, the value we place on our relationships, and how money shapes our lives.

Chapter One

Shakespeare and *The Merchant of Venice*

Shakespeare's References

The Merchant of Venice makes use of several different sources, and, as is typical with Shakespeare's plays, scholars are not in complete agreement on the playwright's references. What everyone agrees about is Shakespeare's ability to take found stories and myths and build something new and complex from them. The three preexisting stories in *The Merchant of Venice* are the ring story, the casket story, and the pound of flesh story.

The casket story plays a prominent role in *The Merchant of Venice*.

The first story relates to rings given with a promise of fidelity, after which that promise is tested. The casket story is a basic fairy-tale model, with a princess, three caskets (boxes that held jewelry or other valuables), and one lucky prince who chooses the right one, thus earning her hand in marriage. The "pound of flesh" story goes back to antiquity, to either India or Persia. It came to Europe in the twelfth century, and wasn't associated with a Jewish person until the thirteenth century, when it first appeared in England. This was when the Jew as "predator/creditor" started to take root as a mythical figure. One clear reference for *The Merchant of Venice* is *Il Pecorone* (*The Simpleton*) from fourteenth-century Italy. This story included the pound of flesh component, as well as a lady with her suitors in Belmont, a promise with a ring, and a Jewish moneylender. Christopher Marlowe's drama *The Jew of Malta* from about 1592 represents another of the more obvious connections. There are many plot parallels between these two works, and even some speeches are similar. The depiction of the titular Jew in Marlowe's play is perhaps the most striking difference, which helps in the analysis of Shylock in Shakespeare's play, because we can see elaborations and departures on his part that were probably done consciously. Whereas Marlowe depicts a caricature—a simple, greedy villain—Shakespeare offers more depth. Marlowe's moneylender does show cleverness and shrewdness, especially early on, but as the play develops, he ends up as a flat character and one to loathe.

Some consider *The Merchant of Venice* to be one of Shakespeare's first "problem plays," in that it presents controversies of his day in ambiguous ways, leaving the thinking audience perplexed. Elizabethans of Shakespeare's time struggled with the balance between justice and mercy in what was a very litigious age, and also with usury, which was moneylending at a high rate of interest. There was a discomfort with this, however, and a common belief that too much of it, charging too high an interest, made the practice evil.

Comedy or Tragedy?

It is difficult to determine whether the play is a comedy or a tragedy. The term comedy implies a neat, tidy plot with a light and happy ending but does not mean that serious themes do not run throughout. A tragedy, on the other hand, may have a messy, unhappy ending and serious commentary on human nature, but this does not preclude the existence of levity. Tragedies tend to follow a trajectory toward death. Comedies may begin with feuding, unhappiness, or confusion, but they end with music and marriage. Young characters often move beyond parental control to a romantic partner.

In *The Merchant of Venice*, we find love, suspense, mixed identities, and a happy ending of sorts, along with many intriguing ambiguities and beautifully astute commentaries on human nature. Is the play purely anti-Semitic? Is Shylock a simplistic "bad guy," or is he a sympathetic character? Is Portia admirable or shallow? Is loyalty absolute or merely relative, and how far should one go to test it?

Anti-Semitism

In terms of anti-Semitism, the play can be difficult for a modern reader to accept, and because of this, *The Merchant of Venice* is one of Shakespeare's most controversial plays. Jewish people recount painful memories of having to read it in school. In 1943, a well-known German actor named Werner Krauss was ordered by Joseph Goebbels, Hitler's minister of propaganda, to play Shylock in such a way as to incite hatred against Jews. Since World War II, the play has been banned from many classrooms. In Shakespeare's day, there was also a strong anti-Jewish sentiment. Venice required Jews to live in a walled area with a gate that locked and was guarded by Christians (the first "ghetto"). If a Jew went out past curfew, he was required to wear a red hat to identify himself. Jews were not allowed to own property.

Shakespeare On-Screen

SHAKESPEARE'S STORIES HAVE been told, retold, and reimagined in movies since the beginning of the film industry. While many early Shakespeare plays found their way onto the big screen without significant changes, movies like *10 Things I Hate About You* and *O* update his work for young adult audiences.

In *10 Things I Hate About You*, Julia Stiles plays Kat, a social outcast whose younger sister Bianca is one of the most popular kids at their California high school. The girls' father is extremely strict and neither one is allowed to date—that is, until their father decides to make an exception as a joke: Bianca can go out on dates as soon as Kat is dating, too. *10 Things I Hate About You* is based on Shakespeare's *The Taming of the Shrew*.

Julia Stiles went on to star in *O* (based on *Othello*) a few years later. *O* also takes place at a high school and tells the story of a star basketball player named Odin who is deeply in love with his classmate Desi. When the coach's son, Hugo, becomes jealous of Odin, Hugo schemes to destroy Odin and Desi's relationship.

Shakespeare's tragedies have also found success on the small screen. *Sons of Anarchy* follows a motorcycle club in present-day California. Jax Teller must navigate the hierarchy of the club following

Heath Ledger and Julia Stiles star in *10 Things I Hate About You*, which is an interpretation of Shakespeare's *The Taming of the Shrew*.

his father's death. At the beginning of the series, Jax's stepfather is club president, but his mother often seems to be pulling the strings. In other words, Jax is a modern-day Hamlet, and he must contend with violence and uncertainty about the meaning of life.

These movies and television shows are just one of the many ways that Shakespeare continues to shape our culture. Shakespeare's influence shows no signs of fading as writers and directors continue to adapt his work.

The character of Shylock (played here by Al Pacino) leads readers to question whether Shakespeare was anti-Semitic or merely criticizing those who are.

Their main source of revenue, usury or moneylending, was technically illegal and was frowned upon as immoral. Using Jews as scapegoats to purge society of fear or unease was not an uncommon phenomenon in Shakespeare's day, and he may have made use of this dramatic situation in order both to appeal to general audiences and also to probe deeper into its origins.

Chapter Two

The Play's
the Thing

Act I, Scene 1

Overview

The opening scene, on a street in Venice, finds Antonio, Salerio, and Solanio talking about Antonio's ships. Antonio is feeling blue, and he doesn't know why. Salerio and Solanio suggest that his ships are worrying him. These friends sympathize with the insecurity of counting on luck and weather, not knowing if one day, circumstances will suddenly change and one's fortunes will shift. "Should I go to church / And see the holy edifice of stone / And not bethink me straight of dangerous rocks, / Which touching but my gentle vessel's side / Would scatter all her spices on the stream, / Enrobe the roaring water with my silks, / And in a word, but even now worth this, / And now worth nothing?"

Venice is the backdrop for much of the play and the bustling city contrasts with Portia's peaceful Belmont.

Antonio assures his friends that his fortunes are not all held in one place, and that this is not why he is sad. The friends' next guess is that he is in love, and he brushes this suggestion off as well. We never discover the actual source of his sadness, which gives this character a vague aimlessness.

Bassanio, Lorenzo, and Gratiano join the group and the mood lifts some. Gratiano notices that Antonio seems out of sorts. He tries to cheer up his friend while playfully goading him. Gratiano talks of supposedly wise men who say very little, but once they do speak, it is revealed that they aren't so wise after all. Lorenzo teases Gratiano for talking so much that he can't get a word in edgewise. The

Gratiano (Aubrey Deeker), disguised as a woman. Shakespeare's fools often wear outlandish costumes.

others leave Antonio and Bassanio alone. First, the two jest about Gratiano's vapid conversation. This character offers a light touch and source of humor, but Shakespeare's "fools" often possess wisdom. Here Antonio's sadness is set aside as soon as he hears about his friend's love affair and his need for a loan.

Bassanio has overspent, and now he needs a decent sum of money in order to woo Portia. He talks of her many virtues (including her wealth), and the sense that he and she have a connection. Without hesitation, Antonio is happy to oblige his dear friend's needs. Because his money is tied up, he will need to use his credit to secure a loan for Bassanio. Here the feeling of unease, of credit stretching too thin, increases, but so do the power and generosity of Antonio's friendship.

Analysis

Antonio's fortunes are unsure or suspended, as they hang in part on his ships completing their journey safely, although he assures his friends that his fortune is well distributed and well protected. Bassanio, who already owes Antonio money, wants to borrow more. This both sets the scene for the central moneylending plot and also brings up the money theme: how much it determines a person's life, happiness, and relationships with others. Money language is used throughout the play.

This scene also explores the value of friendship. The friendship between Antonio and Bassanio is arguably the strongest, most steady relationship in the entire play. Notice how Antonio perks up and drops talk of sadness upon Bassanio's arrival and the chance for him to help his friend. Says Antonio: "My purse, my person my

Antonio (Derek Smith) and Bassanio (Drew Cortese) have a friendship that is complicated by the lending and borrowing of money.

extremest means / Lie all unlock'd to your occasions." Again, friendship accompanies financial offerings. A bit later, when Bassanio worries about the risks Antonio takes in order to offer him the loan he needs, Antonio replies, "To wind about my love with circumstance / And out of doubt you do me now more wrong / In making question of my uttermost / Than if you had made waste of all I have." In other words, his friendship and devoted loyalty are both measured by money and also surpass financial considerations. When Bassanio describes Portia, the word *worth* is also used.

The theme of appearance versus reality is introduced when Antonio comments that the world is "A stage, where every man must play a part, / And mine a sad one." This continues with Gratiano, who plays with words but says nothing—"Gratiano speaks an infinite deal of nothing"—yet he also challenges silence and words, and how those who speak little and are taken as wise might not be.

Act I, Scene 2

Overview

At her house in Belmont, Portia, parallel to Antonio, is feeling inexplicably weary of life. Nerissa, her maid, comments that Portia would truly be unhappy if "your miseries were in the same abundance as your good fortunes are: and yet for aught I see, they are as sick that surfeit with too much, as they that starve with nothing." Here is a lesson as apt today as it was in Shakespeare's day: that those who have too much keep wanting more, and there is a sickness in society from such excess. It's clear the casket competition has grown tedious for Portia.

Nerissa seems to have more faith in the father's wisdom and the happy results of the test. A humorous litany follows, however, of all of the losers who have come to take the test, and luckily for Portia, all will be leaving her soon. Interestingly, it is Nerissa who first brings up Bassanio and describes him as the best choice. Portia agrees.

Analysis

Can money buy happiness? The two wealthiest characters are the two who are the least happy: Antonio and Portia,

Portia lives a life of luxury at her estate at Belmont, depicted here in a painting by William Hodges.

and it is only in giving money away that they gain some contentment. This also overlaps with the theme of appearance versus reality, where characters appear to have everything they wants, and yet still feel dissatisfied.

While Portia acknowledges the wisdom of Nerissa's words about having no reason for sadness, can she act on them? She mentions that it is easier to offer wisdom than follow it; this becomes a stronger issue much later in the play, particularly in the trial scene.

There are two strained father-daughter relationships in this play: that of Portia and her deceased father, and that of Shylock and his daughter, Jessica. In Portia's case, her husband will not be chosen by her, but through a test devised by her father. Here is where the casket story enters. This is the most obvious manifestation of the "appearance versus reality" theme, as her suitors must choose from a gold, silver, or lead casket. The correct guess will bring the reward of Portia's hand in marriage. Portia is resentful of the restriction and is tired of the game.

Act I, Scene 3

Overview

This scene, set at a public place in Venice, starts right in the middle of the action, with Bassanio arranging with Shylock to borrow his wooing money, using Antonio's fortune as collateral. Antonio shows up, and Shylock offers all his hatred in an aside, where he lists what he considers the merchant's offenses. First, Antonio is Christian. Second, he lends money for free and brings down Shylock's rates. Third, he hates all Jews ("our sacred nation"), and he criticizes Shylock's business practices in public. Some bickering follows, during which Shylock proudly cites the Bible and his ancestry, and Antonio shows his impatience. Antonio is starting to feel uneasy and suspicious. The negotiations continue, but when pushed, Shylock complains about the terrible treatment he has had to suffer in the past. Perhaps this is an opening for some kind of sympathy from Antonio, or perhaps this is one more step in the inevitable, entrenched hatred between these two characters. Antonio offers none of the former and plenty of the latter, suggesting that there is no possibility of friendship, so if Shylock is going to lend the money, it may as well be to an enemy and not a friend.

Then comes the brutal bond: Shylock suggests a forfeit of a pound of Antonio's flesh if he does not meet the deadline for repayment. Bassanio is afraid, but Antonio is confident.

Analysis

Although he is not a simple character, Shylock is not easy to like. In this scene, he repeats the amount of the loan, "three thousand ducats," revealing his obsession with money. When he concedes that Antonio is a "good" man, Shylock equates this with his worth instead of his character, offering the word *sufficient* instead and then describing his various assets. Again, appearance versus reality comes into play when Shylock dismisses Antonio's wealth as only virtual or provisional: "Yet his means are in supposition ... ships are but boards, sailors but men, there be land-rats, and water-rats, water-thieves, and land-thieves." Yet doesn't a Jewish businessman need to be cautious and skeptical, given the way he may be judged and discriminated against? There is also a sense throughout the play that, if only Shylock were more "Christian" in his behavior, all would be well. He requests a meeting with Antonio and is invited to dine with Antonio and Bassanio. Perhaps this is merely a well-meaning, friendly gesture, and Shylock's response is exaggerated and bitter. He says, "Yes, to smell pork, to eat of the habitation which your prophet the Nazarite conjured the devil into: I will buy with you, sell with you, talk with you, walk with you, and so following: but I will not eat with you, drink with you, nor pray with you." But maybe, too, the assumption that Shylock can easily fit himself into Christian culture is presumptuous.

Shylock's anger is personal, but he also feels that he represents all Jews: "Cursed be my tribe / If I forgive him!" Some argue that Shylock is a nasty, greedy man, a simple bad guy, and that this is separate from his race. Perhaps he uses his Judaism as an excuse for his self-serving hatred of Antonio. Another argument is that this play is anti-Semitic, and that his greed and hatred are made synonymous with his race. This certainly coincides with common thinking of the time. A third view holds that because of the injustices heaped upon Shylock and his people, he is forced into a defensive and suspicious position, and he must fight against Antonio or else lose his livelihood and his racial pride.

Antonio once again invokes the appearance versus reality theme when he remarks, "The devil can cite scripture for his purpose. An evil soul producing holy witness / Is like a villain with a smiling cheek …" With the talk of friendship, Shylock can play the hurt one, saying that he would have been a friend, if Antonio hadn't "stormed" so. Does he really mean it? Or is he playing up the moment so as better to assert his momentary power?

In Antonio's acceptance of the terms of the loan, we see the power of his friendship with Bassanio and perhaps also his hubris regarding his own luck and fortunes. In both sarcastic bitterness and prophetic wisdom, Antonio comments, "The Hebrew will turn Christian, he grows kind," but Bassanio quips, "I like not fair terms, and a villain's mind." The confusion of suspicion, hatred, and brutality in this exchange foreshadows the trouble to come.

Act II, Scene 1

Overview

We switch back to Belmont and the arrival of the next suitor, with whom we left off when we were last with Portia and Nerissa. The prince of Morocco asks not to be judged by his dark complexion. Portia assures him that even if she were free to choose, as she is not, he would stand as fair a chance as any. The prince is grateful and then eager to pick one of the caskets. He uses courageous, perhaps boastful language to describe his physical, warlike prowess, yet he also admits that all of this is for naught, and one less worthy could simply be luckier in winning what he himself loses: Portia.

Analysis

Here we see the theme of appearance versus reality continue, both with the caskets and the dark-skinned prince. There is some irony that he gets better treatment than Shylock, but he is also a minor character, and, since he loses Portia, he is not a threat to her or her way of life the way Shylock is a threat to the surrounding characters. Destiny plays a role again when the prince juxtaposes his merits against the dumb luck of choosing the right casket. While this frustrates him, perhaps Bassanio and Portia's love is already written in the stars, and no luck, wit, or individual achievements can get in the way of that.

The prince of Morocco (Vinta Morgan) attempts to select the correct casket in exchange for Portia's hand.

Act II, Scene 2

Overview

This scene opens with Launcelot Gobbo, the clown and Shylock's servant, talking to himself on a street in Venice. He wavers back and forth in his decision whether or not to run away, saying how cruel Shylock is, how much like the devil, and yet it is his inner fiend that urges him to run, and his conscience that urges him to stay.

Then Old Gobbo appears, asking directions to Shylock's place. Teasing his near-blind father, Launcelot offers convoluted directions. Old Gobbo asks after Launcelot, and confusion over titles and names ensues, with the son saying he has died, the father sad at the news and not recognizing his son before him. Finally, after some back and forth about Launcelot's beard and how much he has changed, his father acknowledges him. Launcelot is on the run, hoping to switch his services to Bassanio.

Father and son make a tangled offer to Bassanio, both of the gift that was originally meant for Shylock and of Launcelot's services. Bassanio agrees, mentioning that Shylock is also willing to make this switch.

Gratiano shows up as the father and son team are on their way out. He asks to be included in Bassanio's trip to Belmont. Bassanio says that Gratiano's wild and rude ways are fine in his company, but that he must dress and behave with propriety and civility, so that Portia doesn't get the wrong idea about Bassanio. The friends agree that the evening before them is for fun, and that the seriousness will follow. This hints at the more extreme disguised identities in the trial scene.

Analysis

With Launcelot's opening speech, we find a dizzying confusion and are left wondering what is right, what is wrong, and how is one to know? We are also left with a very unfavorable view of Shylock.

Launcelot worries that "I am a Jew if I serve the Jew any longer." He seems to be saying that Judaism is contagious here, and the person with whom one allies oneself is of great importance.

In the conversation with Bassanio, Shylock is equated with being godless or devil-like when Launcelot comments that Bassanio has "the grace of God" while Shylock has "enough." Bassanio is in debt, but he is a gentleman and a Christian. Shylock has wealth, but, as a Jewish person, that is not enough to redeem him; in fact, it becomes a source of criticism (and perhaps jealousy).

Act II, Scene 3

Overview

In Shylock's house, his daughter Jessica says her farewell to Launcelot, sad to see him go, as he added some merriment to a home she says is a hell. They both talk of her "bettering" herself by marrying a Christian. She has sent a note to her beloved, Lorenzo, that the departing servant is meant to deliver in secret. Jessica seems to despise her father, yet acknowledges that a "heinous sin is it in me / To be ashamed to be my father's child!"

Analysis

Jessica gains sympathy from her Christian peers and a Christian audience by criticizing her father and craving escape from his hellish household. It may not be his Judaism, however, that truly troubles her. She is a typical rebellious teen, more bothered perhaps by the "tediousness" (her word)

Shylock's daughter, Jessica, chooses Lorenzo over her faith and family.

of her home than its cultural or religious identity. She doesn't have many choices if she does want to break away, especially since she is in love with Lorenzo, a Christian gentleman. Still her willingness to convert is part of a movement toward a Christian "happily ever after" conclusion, where Shylock is forced to do so as well.

Act II, Scene 4

Overview

Gratiano, Lorenzo, Salerio, and Solanio discuss preparations for the upcoming party or "masque," which includes elaborate costumes. Launcelot delivers Jessica's letter, and Lorenzo recognizes her handwriting. Lorenzo sends Launcelot back to Jessica with the reply that he will not fail her. While Salerio and Solanio head off to prepare for the festivities, Gratiano and Lorenzo talk about Jessica. Lorenzo shares the plans that Jessica has just set out: She asks that Lorenzo carry her off from her father's home, and she will bring with her all the gold and jewels that she can.

Analysis

Here begins the sequence of disguises and hidden or confused identities, which is part of the appearance versus reality theme. With the loving couples in the play, it seems each person in the relationship is able to see below the surface of the other. Here, the exterior is an envelope, and for Bassanio, it will be the caskets.

Once again, romance goes hand in hand with money. Does Jessica become more appealing because she has wealth to bring with her, or does she feel pressure to do so? Jessica's betrayal of her father is excused by the characters in the play because of his religion. "And never dare misfortune cross her foot, / Unless she do it under this excuse, / That she is issue to a faithless Jew."

Act II, Scene 5

Overview

Launcelot visits Shylock, his old boss, to invite him to dine with Bassanio, his new master. Shylock is grumpy and grudging in his assent, saying that the invitation does not come from friendship: "I am not bid for love, they flatter me. / But yet I'll go in hate." He is especially hesitant because of a dream he had, about moneybags, which causes him worry and Launcelot mirth; he mocks Shylock's superstition.

Shylock asks Jessica to watch the house and keep it locked up, and not even to look out at the foolish Christians and their partying. Launcelot whispers to Jessica about her escape plan and Lorenzo's visit.

After Launcelot's departure, Shylock explains why he is glad to be rid of him. He says that this servant was slow and lazy, "snail-slow in profit" and wishes that he will end up wasting the money of his new master instead, who happens also to be the benefactor of Shylock's loan, Bassanio. Shylock leaves, and Jessica is alone with her excitement and anxiety over her plan to run away from home.

Analysis

In his response to the dinner invitation, Shylock shows himself to be either a bitter, unpleasant man who always expects the worst of people, or someone who is used to being treated with mistrust, insincerity, and bigotry, and knows better than to expect friendship. Is he being unfair and paranoid when he asks Jessica to lock all doors and not even to peep out? Certainly not, because when he is not in earshot, Launcelot advises Jessica to do the opposite of her father's bidding, to be on the lookout for a certain Christian gentleman who plans to "rescue" her.

In this scene, the obsession with money resurfaces and the controversy continues. Is Shylock unbearably miserly and greedy, or necessarily thrifty and cautious? The proverb that he quotes, "Fast bind, fast find—A proverb never stale in thrifty mind," could be interpreted either way. He has worked hard to earn, save, and maintain his fortune. It is all he has. And yet maybe he needs to appreciate other things, especially his own daughter, who at that very moment is plotting to leave him.

Act II, Scene 6

Overview

The scene continues in front of Shylock's house, where Gratiano and Salerio await Lorenzo, wondering why he is late. If he is pursuing love, shouldn't he be early, not late? Lorenzo apologizes when he arrives, claiming, "Not I, but my affairs, have made you wait."

Lorenzo approaches Shylock's house, and Jessica calls down to him. She asks who is there, but recognizes his voice, and they both exchange vows of love. Jessica is glad to be clothed in night, embarrassed by her forward words, and also embarrassed by her disguise in boy's clothes (this foreshadows Portia and Nerissa's later disguise). Lorenzo is

Jessica (Amelia Pedlow) runs away with Lorenzo (Matthew Carlson), bringing along her father's money and her mother's ring.

not bothered by either, and he welcomes her to join him. Jessica does not come empty-handed; she brings along a significant amount of her father's wealth.

Gratiano approves of Jessica. Lorenzo then outlines his judgment of her, that she has proven herself to be fair, wise, and true—but, while she may be true to him, she certainly is not true to her father or her heritage.

Antonio appears and announces that there won't be a party after all, and that Bassanio is ready to set sail. Gratiano says he is pleased to get going.

Analysis

Interestingly, as she joins Lorenzo, Jessica says, "I will make fast the doors, and gild myself / With some more ducats," as if she herself is golden, as if she is worthier of love because of the money she carries. Gratiano is impressed, calling Jessica "gentle" (also a pun with the word *gentile*) and "no Jew," so for her to count as a viable mate for his friend, as a respectable woman, she cannot also be Jewish. Most of the obviously anti-Semitic comments come from minor characters, with the exception of Antonio. This could be Shakespeare's way of dismissing or critiquing such sentiments, juxtaposing them against more subtle and tolerant views.

Earlier, Gratiano was happy about the party or masque. Now he is happy not to go, because Bassanio is on his way to Belmont (where, it will turn out, Nerissa is waiting for Gratiano).

Act II, Scene 7

We switch back again to Portia and the prince of Morocco, which draws out the suspense of his task. Now the time has come for him to choose a casket. He passes up the lead one, as the inscription announces, "Who chooseth me must give and hazard all he hath." Why take risks merely for lead? The prince esteems himself quite highly, better than lead. The silver casket tempts him. "Who chooseth me, shall get as much as he deserves." He convinces himself that in fortune, breeding and love, he surely does deserve this lady. He takes a look at the gold one, and finds, "Who chooseth me shall gain what many men desire," and is sure that men the world over desire Portia. He then makes the mistake of equating the woman with outward appearances and the materials of the boxes, and decides that lead and silver are not worthy of her.

Morocco opens the casket to find a skull and a scroll. The often-quoted proverb begins the note: "All that glisters (glitters) is not gold." The note continues to berate him for being more bold than wise. With deep sadness and disappointment, the prince rushes off.

Analysis

This scene builds up the suspense and moves the fairy tale forward. Three suitors will try the test and the magic number three will mark the victor. We also see the theme of appearance versus reality shine forth. For Morocco, the outward appearances of the caskets carry too much meaning. After his departure, Portia comments again about his "complexion." Is she snidely canceling her earlier assurance of not being bothered by his dark skin? There is a hint of this, a hint that her words do not always reflect her true feelings. This is another version of that same theme, the surface of words, opposed to the hidden meanings below them. Shakespeare toys with this throughout the play.

Act II, Scene 8

Overview

Back in Venice, we are thrust into the middle of the action again, with Salerio and Solanio discussing Jessica's escape. Bassanio's ship was under suspicion, but Antonio vouched for him that Jessica was not on board. The Duke of Venice was informed that the two lovers were spotted in a gondola. Shylock's response is reported and critiqued. He yells "My daughter! O my ducats! O my daughter! / Fled with a Christian! O my Christian ducats!"

Salerio prophetically remarks, "Let good Antonio look he keep his day, / Or he shall pay for this," demonstrating that Shylock's rage and later vengeful resolve do indeed stem from the hurt and anger over this betrayal. They discuss some bad shipping news and worry about Antonio's fortunes. Salerio then reports what a kind and loyal friend Antonio is, that he generously suggested that Bassanio spend as long as he wants with the woman he loves and not even think about his friend's bond, and that they shook hands as Antonio fought back tears. These two men admire Antonio and look out for him, wishing him the best and hoping to keep him in good cheer.

On one level, the daughter and ducat quote indicates that Shylock is obsessed with money (but do keep in mind that this is a secondhand report, not spoken directly by him), as worried about his money as his daughter. But on another level, the fact that his daughter has run off with a Christian is a blow to his entire faith, and the depletion of his funds—the only source of respect and power that he has—marks a loss that is more than just monetary.

Antonio is presented as a contrast to Shylock—he is loyal to a fault and confident of his fortunes, while Shylock is alone, recently bereft of daughter and jewels, ungenerous and cautious with his wealth. That these two characters are opposites and enemies, and that both make mistakes of extremity, serves as a call for balance.

Act II, Scene 9

Overview

At Belmont we are already on to the next prince, Arragon, and Portia is called quickly to witness his performance. Portia and Arragon review the rules of the "competition." Quickly he dismisses the lead box and, soon after, the gold one. He says that "many men" would include too wide a group, fools who judge only by their eyes. He does not want to be ranked among the common masses. The silver box is his choice. He seems sure that many do not earn their titles or truly deserve Portia, but he does. Unfortunately for him, this turns out not to be the case. He finds there a picture of a fool. Shocked, he asks if this is really what he

ARCHAND DE VENISE. Le prince d'Aragon, refusé comme prétendant.

VÉRITABLE EXTRAIT DE VIANDE LIEBIG.

The prince of Arragon incorrectly chooses the silver casket.

deserves. Portia replies with another proverb, "To offend and judge are distinct offices, / And of opposed natures." Judgment should be neutral, wise, and free of bias, anger, or frustration. Arragon, Morocco, and others like them are short on wisdom and, therefore, their judgments are suspect. Arragon rushes off in embarrassment.

Portia is tired and irritated with her suitors thus far, saying their losses are their own fault, that their lack of wisdom ends up leading them to frustration. Nerissa replies that destiny is what really determines the outcome, and then, as timing would have it, the next suitor's arrival is announced. (It is Bassanio.) It soon will be his turn to test his destiny. The messenger describes the suitor with great enthusiasm. Portia cuts him off, wishing to view this new suitor. Nerissa follows, secretly hoping it is Bassanio.

Analysis

Arragon perhaps does a bit better than Morocco, showing understanding of the "all that glitters is not gold" proverb without having to encounter it, and yet, it is his pride in himself, not his appreciation of Portia, that moves him to reject the golden casket.

While the suitors who seem fixated on appearance lose the contest, Bassanio is appreciated partly because of his rich appearance. The messenger equates his wealth with his worthiness when he says, "… Gifts of rich value; / yet I have not seen so likely an ambassador of love." In her impatience Portia reveals a similar bias: "I long to see / Quick Cupid's post that comes so mannerly." Nerissa is excited, too, and hopes the suitor is Bassanio. Just as Gratiano approved of Jessica, here Nerissa welcomes Bassanio as Portia's possible spouse. The judgment of friends is a nice, perhaps needed, affirmation.

Act III, Scene 1

Overview

In Venice, Salerio and Solanio talk about the loss of one of Antonio's ships, just as they had foretold in the very first scene. There is also some levity with puns and jokes about gossipy or untrustworthy women and a play on the word end, with Salerio asking his friend to get to the end of his point, and the other replying that he hopes this marks the *end* of Antonio's losses. They note the arrival of Shylock with unpleasant dread, "Let me say amen betimes, lest the devil cross my prayer, for here he comes in the likeness of a Jew."

Shylock angrily confronts these two with the fact that they knew about his daughter's escape. Again, while the exchange is about a serious, emotional topic, there is playfulness in the language. Solanio comments that Jessica was full-grown (a bird full fledged) and ready to go. There is a play on the words *dam* and *damned*, with Shylock saying she will be damned for this. Then, when he comments on her being his flesh and blood, Solanio teases him by reinterpreting that expression in sexual terms, saying Shylock is too old for that. Salerio comments that Shylock and Jessica are more different than alike (leading again to her acceptance in the Christian world). To add to the animosity and frustration, he taunts Shylock with a question about Antonio's ships.

Shylock shows suspicion at not having seen Antonio lately, and in his already angry state, rants and raves about Antonio and his smugness, and says that the bond will be honored. Salerio pushes Shylock even further when he says that there is certainly no use in actually holding Antonio to his agreement and taking a pound of his flesh. Then follows one of the most famous speeches in the play, when Shylock explains his motivation in following through with the once "merry" agreement. Antonio has mocked him, hurt his business, criticized his entire race ("scorned my nation"), turned his friends from him, and all because he is a Jew. He has eyes, hands, organs, all the same parts as Christians. If a Christian is wronged, he'll seek vengeance, so why can't a Jew do the same?

A messenger then appears to call Solanio and Salerio to Antonio's house. When Tubal, Shylock's friend, arrives, Solanio makes another reference to the devil: "Here comes another of the tribe—a third cannot be match'd, unless the devil himself turn Jew."

Shylock asks Tubal about Jessica and receives only bad news. She cannot be found. Shylock expresses great anger and frustration, perhaps masking hurt, saying he would rather she were dead at his feet than escaped with his jewels. He bemoans the loss of money both with her escape and with the efforts to find her. The good news is that one of Antonio's ships was lost. Shylock actually thanks God for this, which does not make him look very good. Tubal then offers more painful news about Jessica, that she is spending wildly, and actually traded the ring of beloved Leah, Shylock's deceased wife, for a monkey. Tubal ends by cheering Shylock up with a reminder that Antonio, too, has suffered a loss, and will likely not be able to return the loan. Shylock is glad of this and is spurred to action, setting a plan in motion and commenting that with Antonio out of the way, his business will thrive.

Analysis

Throughout the play, Shylock is associated with the devil, and here we see that in very unsubtle terms. The separation of Jessica from Shylock pushes plot and thematic elements. It allows her to move closer to the Christian world, as highlighted here by Salerio's comment that father and daughter do not seem to be of the same blood. It also provides the primary motivation for Shylock to take the bond literally and seek vengeance against Antonio. The merchant had already represented more than a commercial rival for Shylock. As someone who spat upon and looked down on Shylock, he represents all Christians who won't accept Shylock or any Jewish person. At the same time, this becomes not just general, but very personal, because of the loss of Shylock's daughter. Solanio and Salerio's taunts, as well as Tubal's news about the lost ship, are all that Shylock needs to combine all of his rage and pain in the pursuit of his bond. Oddly, he uses the word *vengeance* when he talks of Jessica. His speech here is disturbing, as he spends more time talking about the financial loss associated with her departure and the efforts to find her than the loss of his daughter. Shylock seems to think only of money, and at the same time, he looks not just at its face value, but at what it represents: power, security, and loyalty. Jessica betrayed him in two ways, first by running away with a Christian, thus denying her father and her heritage; and second by absconding with much of his wealth.

Shylock offers the powerful speech in this scene that is a primary source of sympathy for him, and yet he still does not come across so well. He seems unable to address the deep and personal pain of the loss of his daughter and instead focuses on financial issues. He mentions God only when thankful of Antonio's predicament, and decides to meet at the synagogue not to worship, but to make plans for Antonio's destruction. Even that plan is not discussed in terms of retribution for terrible, racist wrongs, but in mercantile terms. It would be good for business. It could be spirituality in general that is at stake here, however, not merely Shylock's faith. In the "Hath not a Jew eyes?" speech, Shylock mentions that Christians and Jews alike seek vengeance.

Act III, Scene 2

Overview

Back at Belmont, Portia and Bassanio are together, and yet they are not. He has to pass the test first. She gives a long speech about wanting to stall the process, because she might lose him, while before he takes the test, at least he is with her. She apologizes for talking so much, yet does so. She bemoans the fact that she has to follow rules and cannot be completely his.

She is tempted to break the rules but does not. Bassanio cannot wait, however. The suspense is agonizing for him. Portia then expresses suspicion and misgivings. "Upon the rack Bassanio? Then confess / What treason there is mingled with your love." He assures her that his love is true and pure, and she is appeased. Portia then requests music as background to his endeavor. Depending on the outcome, the music can play a different role. It can add to the mood of sadness and defeat if he loses, her tears mingling with the tune, or if he wins, it will be wedding music.

The little tune that she sings along to happens to have end rhymes that rhyme with "lead." She could be offering a sneaky clue for Bassanio here, or else the hint is for the audience.

Bassanio (Drew Cortese) embraces his wife-to-be, Portia (Julia Coffey), after selecting the lead casket.

Bassanio then speaks of outward courage, outward beauty which mask the opposite. He is not moved by the "gaudy gold," but instead goes for the lead casket, which does not offer gifts, but asks that the one selecting it be the giver.

In an aside, Portia is ecstatic, overwhelmed by her own emotions. All petty feelings that tarnish love, such as jealousy, fear, or despair, vanish. Bassanio opens the casket to find a picture of Portia. He is the winner! First he praises the picture, and wonders how the artist could have done such a good job, especially with her eyes. Wouldn't viewing one entrance him so that he couldn't finish the other one? But then Bassanio notes that the real Portia puts the picture to shame. The scroll inside congratulates him for seeing past surface appearances, asks him to accept his prize and look no further, and grants him permission to kiss his bride. Bassanio cannot believe his good luck and needs the kiss to confirm that it is true.

Portia says she is not worthy of him, and wishes she was much more, but is willing to learn from him and do her best to please him. She says that all that is hers is now his, and offers him her ring, saying that parting from it means parting from her and life. Bassanio takes the ring and accepts the promise.

Gratiano then asks permission also to be wed. He has already found Nerissa. They apparently have made a deal that if Bassanio won Portia's hand, Nerissa would give herself to Gratiano. Portia asks her maid if this is indeed true, and Nerissa confirms the agreement. Nerissa and Gratiano have Portia and Basssanio's blessings. Then, Lorenzo, Jessica, and Salerio appear.

Bassanio receives a letter from Antonio with very bad news. Portia notices her lover's pale face and knows this before hearing it. Antonio's ships have all faltered, and Shylock is not interested in the money anyway. He is insisting that the bond be honored. Bassanio admits to

Portia with shame that he not only "was nothing" as he had said when wooing her, but less than that, because he was in debt to Antonio. Portia immediately asks how much is owed, offers to pay twenty times that, and says that, after their marriage, Bassanio should take her money and go fix this problem, while she and Nerissa will wait virtuously at a local monastery (living as "maids and widows").

Portia asks to hear the letter. Bassanio reads aloud that Antonio expects to die, and only requests one last chance to see Bassanio, but only if Bassanio himself truly wants to, only if he truly loves Antonio. Portia urges Bassanio to go and see Antonio, and he is off, promising his loyalty to her as he goes.

Analysis

Portia plays the coy, submissive lady here, yet contradicts such an image at the same time. She apologizes for talking too much, but does so anyway. She claims a passive obedience to her father's dictated casket trick, yet offers a clue to Bassanio through the background song. She describes herself as unworthy of Bassanio, yet is quick to use her wealth to fix Antonio's problem. Oddly, she says, "Since you are dear bought, I will love you dear." This could simply mean that it was so difficult to finally get Bassanio as her husband, that she treasures him even more. *Dear* is another money term, though, as is *bought*, of course. Portia seems unabashed about her wealth and what it means and brings her.

There is disagreement among scholars about Lorenzo and Jessica's arrival, since she is not given a greeting. Some note a disruption of the lines' rhythm, which could indicate editing and lost versions, or else lines have been dropped to keep the action moving quickly. A third interpretation is that Jessica, still a Jewish person and therefore an outsider, is ignored by all, especially Portia. Gratiano does refer to her as an "infidel."

Act III, Scene 3

Overview

Antonio with the jailer (Gaoler) encounters a very angry Shylock on a street in Venice. Antonio tries to start up a conversation with Shylock, but Shylock will not have it. He simply repeats the refrain that he will have his bond. Antonio then backs off, saying it is useless to try to reason with Shylock. Solanio tries to reassure him, saying the duke would never let the terrible bond go through, but Antonio replies that the law must be honored. Venice relies on the international world of business, and therefore, must adhere to laws and apply those to all concerned, or else these commercial connections will be destroyed.

Analysis

In one interpretation, Shylock is sinking toward madness, and thus we see his usual speech pattern of rhythmic prose with repetition go further, into almost senseless repetition: "I'll have my bond." Perhaps he can't even hear Antonio at this point. Another view would hold that his built-up anger from being mistreated by everyone has now found its focus and release, so he is bent on vengeance against Antonio, the spokesperson or representative of those injustices.

Antonio also, of course, ruins Shylock's business, as he himself points out here: "I oft deliver'd from his forfeitures / Many that have at times made moan to me, / Therefore he hates me." Yet is it Antonio who is oversimplifying? Shylock earlier says, "Thou call'dst me dog before thou hadst a cause, / But since I am a dog, beware my fangs," touching on the self-fulfilling prophecy often found in racist environments. If a group is assumed to be a certain way, individuals within that group sometimes feel trapped by that expectation, and end up giving in to it.

Antonio foresees his own doom by describing the necessary inflexibility of the law. Antonio seems resigned to his death, and what is most important to him is Bassanio. "—pray God Bassanio come / To see me pay his debt, and then I care not." Interestingly, he does not discuss justice, but business, saying that the commercial welfare of Venice depends on these laws. "For the commodity that strangers have / With us in Venice, if it be denied, / Will much impeach the justice of his state."

Act III, Scene 4

Overview

At Portia's home, she and Lorenzo swap praises. He talks of her noble character and deeds, and she replies that she does not turn away from good deeds. She talks of wanting to help when she can, and of how pleased she is to help Antonio, who, as Bassanio's friend, must be a great person. She says that one wants to spend time with people of high quality. She pulls back then, not wanting to brag, and lays out her false plan to leave her residence for quiet contemplation while Lorenzo and Jessica will be in charge of Belmont.

Next, Portia gives instructions to Balthazar, saying that he has always been trustworthy and she hopes he will continue to be so. He is to visit her cousin, Doctor Bellario, with her message and meet her in Venice with clothes and notes from Bellario. She gives Nerissa hints of the plan that she has clearly already fully developed, but uses playful, tricky language, mentioning that they will see their husbands sooner than expected, that the husbands will see them but not know them. She talks of becoming men, and offers a bawdy caricature of what it means to be a man. Nerissa asks what this is all about, and Portia offers to fill her in offstage, allowing some suspense for the audience.

Analysis

Who can you trust, what do surface appearances reveal, and who is really running the show? This scene raises all of these questions. The theme of judging others by the company they keep continues here, as Portia says any friend of Bassanio's is a friend of hers. She makes it clear that only the "right sort" should spend time together, which heightens Shylock's exclusion. Portia rushes to action, soon to be the most dramatic, plot-turning action in the play.

Act III, Scene 5

Overview

This light scene offers much wordplay and establishes Jessica and Lorenzo as the temporary proprietors of

Belmont. They do not have the status or grace of Portia and Bassanio, however, as shown in the circular, unserious language and in Launcelot's teasing of Jessica. He fears that she cannot avoid being damned, as the daughter of a Jew, and even being "saved" by her husband and converting is not a good thing, because one less Jew drives up the price of pork. Still, there is merriment and love, with talk of the upcoming meal and Jessica and Lorenzo's mutual admiration.

Analysis

The most harshly anti-Semitic comments are hidden in comedy, which perhaps makes them less credible but nonetheless present. That Jessica can only be a stand-in mistress, a false and temporary one, clearly shows her lower status. Here, to be virtuous or "Christian" is also to be a "bastard," meaning that her father is not her real father, which, of course, would speak badly of her mother, or else her father would be the wronged one.

Notice, too, how this is reinforced by her praises for Portia, whom, she says, has no one equal. Indirectly she is putting herself down. Instead of immediately praising his new wife, Lorenzo instead assures her that he is Portia's equal. In a way, following the theme that our value comes from the company we keep, he is assuring her of her value or status, but at the same time, she does not get recognition here. When they joke about praises at the dinner table, the focus is still on her praising him instead of the other way around.

When Launcelot plays around with Lorenzo, he is intentionally misunderstanding a simple request to call people to dinner, but at the same time, showing his cleverness with language and the emptiness of such cleverness: "The fool hath planted in his memory / An army of good words, and I do know / A many fools that stand in better place, / Garnish'd like him, that for a tricksy word / Defy the matter." In a play where characters' hypocrisies are hinted at and critiqued, the fool or clown here reminds us to be suspicious of words, and to look below their surface.

Act IV, Scene 1

Overview

The duke and Antonio enter the Venetian courtroom with their attendants, discussing Shylock's angry inflexibility and Antonio's resignation. Antonio acknowledges the duke's good but unsuccessful efforts to dissuade his adversary. The duke then calls for Shylock. The duke tries one more time, saying to the moneylender that both he and everyone else expect Shylock to change his mind, to back down at the last minute, to show sympathy for Antonio and his unfortunate commercial losses, and not only to dismiss the cruel bond, but forgive at least part of the loan. Shylock refuses. He says he has the legal right to claim the bond, and if this is not honored, the city's standing and freedom are at risk. He then addresses the cruelty and irrationality of his bond. He argues that he need not offer any reason at all, and has every right to follow his emotions, that people have irrational fear or hatreds of rats, pigs or cats, so he can feel that way about Antonio.

Bassanio takes up the argument, saying that Shylock's reasons aren't good and asking why should he kill what he doesn't love. Shylock has no interest in pleasing Bassanio,

The duke (*right*, Drew Eshelman) tries to convince Shylock to renounce his bond, but Shylock will not be swayed.

retorting that no one would hate something and not want to kill it. Antonio, in his mood of resignation, tells Bassanio not to bother, that Shylock will not budge, and is in fact as unchangeable as nature—a wolf, the wind. Shylock reminds everyone that it is not even about money anymore, and if he had six times the amount, he would still not back down.

The duke introduces the idea of mercy, saying that Shylock can expect none if he offers none. Shylock says he is doing nothing wrong, that he is simply honoring the law, and he reminds all of those gathered that they buy slaves, thus exchanging human lives for money, and that he only purchased one pound of human flesh. To accept slavery means they must accept his action, or else their laws fall apart. The duke says he waits for Doctor Bellario, and Salerio mentions the arrival of a messenger. Bassanio tells Antonio not to lose hope, and that he would give up his own flesh and blood rather than let Antonio be harmed. Still Antonio feels lost, saying that Bassanio's best task now will be to write his epitaph.

The dramatic tension builds and builds, as Nerissa arrives, disguised as a young lawyer's assistant, and Shylock sharpens his knife. Bassanio and Gratiano talk to Shylock, criticizing him for his cruelty, which is harder and sharper than his knife. Like Antonio, Gratiano calls Shylock inhuman and wolflike. Shylock quips that Gratiano is wasting his breath, unless he can disprove the legality of the bond. Meanwhile, the duke receives Bellario's letter, which talks of his illness and the young lawyer (Portia in disguise) whom he recommends in his place.

Portia enters, asks for "the merchant" and "the Jew," and then affirms that Shylock does indeed have a legal right to claim his bond. Swiftly, though, she turns to him and says that he must be merciful. Shylock asks why he should. Portia then offers one of her most famous speeches, explaining the heavenly quality of mercy, a gift that is given yet grows, something that is godlike and separate from courtroom technicalities or earthly pettiness. Justice can't bring salvation, but mercy can.

Shylock is still unmoved, insisting on the law. Portia asks about the loan, and Bassanio pleads with her to

Portia (Julia Coffey) and Nerissa (Liz Wisan) scheme to dress as a lawyer and his assistant in order to resolve the court case in their favor.

accept as much as ten times the original amount from him—anything to call off Shylock. Portia stays with the law, gaining Shylock's admiration and drawing out the agony and fear in all the others. She does try to offer Shylock three times the original amount, and he refuses. Portia tells Shylock to get ready to claim his bond, and perhaps baiting him while preparing for her final trick, asks that he not let Antonio bleed to death. Shylock points out that this detail is not stated directly in the bond. So, the bond must be taken literally, and soon this will be to Portia's advantage. Antonio seems ready to die, saying that at least he can go before having to grow old and poor and saying that he truly loved Bassanio and has no regrets about dying for him.

Bassanio answers that, as much as he loves his wife, he would give her up and his own life, too, to save Antonio. Portia, in not a very lawyerly manner, chides Bassanio, saying that his wife, if she were here, would not like to hear that. Then Gratiano joins in, saying the same about Nerissa. In an aside Shylock says that he is the only one bothered by this, besides the wives, and says that if these are Christians, he would not want his daughter stuck with such people.

Portia moves on, saying that Shylock may now take his pound of flesh. At the last minute, she holds him off and goes back to the wording of the bond. Since it only mentions flesh, not blood, he would have to take one without shedding a drop of the other. If he does so (which, of course, could not be avoided) he would lose all of his land and money to the state. Basically, she says: "You wanted justice? Well, now you get it." Shylock goes back to the original offer of three times the loan, and Bassanio

The judge rules that Shylock (Mark Nelson) may take his pound of flesh, but only if he does not spill a drop of Antonio's (Derek Smith) blood.

is ready to comply, but Portia won't have it. She says that Shylock must go through with the original claim, cutting the flesh, and shedding no blood, or else he dies and loses everything. Shylock wants to give up now, but there is more. Portia brings out another law, one about aliens intending to cause the death of a citizen. To comply with

The ring Portia (Rachel Pickup) gives to Bassanio (Daniel Lapaine) represents loyalty. While Portia is dressed as a lawyer, she attempts to test his loyalty by asking for the ring.

that law, Shylock must give half of his goods to the victim and half to the state.

The duke steps in and is the first to offer some mercy in this scene, saying that Shylock may keep his life and that the half due to the state may be commuted to a fine. Shylock says that he might as well die. If his entire livelihood is taken away, he loses his life anyway.

Portia now asks Antonio about mercy. Antonio complies, saying that the half due to him should go instead to Lorenzo and Jessica, upon Shylock's death. There is one more stipulation: that Shylock convert to Christianity. The duke agrees that this is the only thing that would earn Shylock any leniency at this point. Shylock agrees, but immediately asks to be dismissed, as he is not well.

Now the others can celebrate. The duke invites the disguised Portia to dine with him, but she says she must go. Bassanio and Antonio praise and thank her, and offer to pay her for her services, but she declines. After some back and forth, she asks for a small token, the ring on Bassanio's finger. He tries to say no, but she acts insulted and Antonio urges him on, so he finally does part with it.

Analysis

This is the climax of the play, where all of the themes unite in intense and suspenseful action. According to some, Shylock has gone mad with grief at the loss of his daughter. This is why his speech is repetitive, why he can't listen to others, why even money does not speak to him, only vengeance. When Shylock is urged to offer a gentle answer, his angry response shows his increasing madness, the fact that he is trapped by his own worst instincts. Notice how he says "… Must yield to such inevitable shame / As to offend, himself being offended," implying that what he has to do is shameful to himself. He wishes it were otherwise, but it is too late now. He also says that he follows a "losing suit." He probably foresees his own destruction, more like a tragic hero than a comic villain. The course has been set, and he cannot stop it.

Shylock is not a simple greedy Jew caricature, or else he would have taken the money and run. His inflexibility is startling and cruel, but his isolation is also striking. He is alone in a Christian world, with a chorus of baiters and haters throughout the scene. Even the duke's request for a "gentle" response indicates this, with the pun on the word *Gentile* (meaning "non-Jewish"). The only way for him to be acceptable is to be Christian, and at the end, becoming a Christian is part of his punishment. The Christian view of mercy is thrust upon him. Portia as the lawyer says he "must" show mercy, but he is right to point out that in a court of law, there is no compulsion for such gestures. Later on, he is not able to offer what she has demanded of him. Once the flaw in the bond is pointed out, Bassanio is ready to offer Shylock the money and be done with it, but she won't stop at that. She forces his doom and humiliation.

The money theme runs throughout this exciting scene as well. Interestingly, in his sad, dying speech, Antonio says that at least he can die young and wealthy instead of old and poor. Shylock, the supposedly money-obsessed character, will not be bought in this scene. Yet when his worldly goods are taken from him, he says that he may as well be dead. Bassanio offers bold, impulsive gifts to save his friend, which is similar to Antonio's generosity at the beginning of the play (although it is Portia's money with which he is being so generous).

Portia (Geraldine James) outwits Shylock (Dustin Hoffman) in the courtroom scene.

Loyalty and friendship are also explored. Antonio is willing to die for his friend. Portia tests her new husband's loyalty with the ring, and he fails. The triangular situation is heightened when Antonio pretty much asks Bassanio to choose him over his wife (but he also includes the lawyer on his side, and this lawyer, of course, is actually Bassanio's wife): "Let his deservings and my love withal / Be valued 'gainst your wife's commandment."

Shylock is friendless. His love for his daughter is displayed when he comments that she deserves a better husband than these Christians who forsake their wives for friends. Antonio is ready to die at the beginning of the scene, and keeps confirming this in each subsequent speech. Is this because the one he loves is taken? He is happier to die for Bassanio than continue living with him married to Portia. Or it could also be because he has lost the battle against his hate. This kind, generous merchant hates Shylock with the fierce, irrational, animal hate that Shylock feels for him, and he cannot live that way. In a way, Antonio can resolve his hate by offering Christian mercy and bringing Shylock (actually, forcing him) into his faith. To Shylock, however, this kind of inviting inclusion is painful, not celebratory.

Act IV, Scene 2

Overview

In this brief scene, Portia and Nerissa head toward Shylock's house, so he can sign the deed. Gratiano catches up with them to hand over Bassanio's ring. Portia asks that he thank Bassanio for her, and Nerissa suggests to Portia that she, too, will try to get the promised ring away from her husband. Portia confidently declares that they will outwit their husbands.

Analysis

When Portia says, "That cannot be" to the dinner invitation, she may also be expressing dismay that her husband did actually give up the ring. Still, she never loses her composure or is without a plan, and immediately is ready for the next stage of the plot of disguise and trickery, assuring Nerissa that they will "outface them, and outswear them too." Once again, friendship is more reliable than love as Nerissa immediately agrees to follow her friend and mistress with the test of loyalty, risking the same disappointment in her own husband as Portia has just had to endure.

Act V, Scene 1

Overview

Lorenzo and Jessica enjoy the bucolic, romantic setting of Belmont, in stark contrast to the tense, gritty courtroom scene in Venice. They talk of love, but in a teasing way, mentioning famous pairs of lovers, but those known for difficult affairs with questions of loyalty. Lorenzo mentions Jessica in the third person, as if she is one from that list, and she adds that Lorenzo won Jessica with untrue vows of love. A messenger interrupts their playfulness to announce the arrival of Portia. Launcelot shows up and delivers a goofy version of the same message, that his master (Bassanio) is also on his way back. Lorenzo at first wants to rush in and get ready for their arrival, but then decides that they can enjoy the night a bit longer, and requests music to add to the lovely mood. He talks of the merits of music. Jessica says that music does not make her happy. Lorenzo goes on to discuss the taming and magical effects of music, and that a person who is not moved by music should not be trusted.

Portia and Nerissa arrive, note the music and how good it sounds at night, and Lorenzo recognizes Portia's voice. She is told that Bassanio is also on his way back. Then the husbands arrive, and immediately after everyone greets one another, the wives ask about the rings, first Nerissa, and then Portia (after saying that her husband would never give it away). The women first say they will not enter their husband's beds until they see the rings, and then they reveal that they have the rings, but still don't give up the whole game, instead claiming that they have slept with the lawyer and his clerk (which of course they have, because they are these characters). As with the trial scene, there is long drawn-out suspense from intentional wordplay, but here the mood is light and teasing. Finally the women tell the whole story, and the amazed husbands are happy and hugely relieved. To add to the happiness, Antonio gets the news that his ships are actually fine, and Lorenzo and Jessica receive the news of their inheritance (from Shylock's penalty). The couples go off for the evening, and all is well, at least in Belmont.

Analysis

Although this is the happy ending, the play is not a simple comedy. For a tidy wrap-up, Shylock would need to have been dispensed with lightly, either mocked as a completely ridiculous character, or turned around to the "good side." His sad departure from the courtroom and the ambivalent "goodness" of those who heckled and derided him do not offer this tidiness. The love, harmony, and music in the last act also are not pure or simple. The poetry that Lorenzo offers is indeed mellifluous and lovely, but he describes uncomfortable loves. When he includes Jessica in the list, he says, "In such a night / Did Jessica steal from the wealthy Jew, / And with an unthrift love did run from Venice," once again mixing money with love. The word steal can mean "sneak," as in "steal away," yet also, of course, it means taking money or goods from someone, which is what Jessica did to Shylock. They tease one another about not meaning their vows, and with the trick of the rings, loyalty again is being challenged. Jessica is not merry at the sound of music. This could make her untrustworthy, as Lorenzo says those who don't like music are, or it could show her unease at what she has done, her inability to rejoice completely.

Portia is the witty trickster, the mistress of all the joy in Belmont. Antonio says to her, "Sweet lady, you have given me life and living; / For here I read for certain that my ships / Are safely come to road," and Lorenzo comments, "Fair ladies, you drop manna in the way / Of starved people." Money is really the hero here, though. Antonio's "life and living" are associated with his returned wealth, and Lorenzo's joy also comes from the same source. They all have won and Shylock has lost in terms of finances, and in one sense, that is what truly counts in this world.

Open-Source
Shakespeare

IN 2012, THE Folger Shakespeare Library announced an ambitious project called the Folger Digital Texts. Full versions of every Shakespeare play are at your fingertips on the site—for free. But two features set the Folger Digital Texts website apart from others sites hosting Shakespeare texts, like Project Gutenberg or Google Books. First, the Folger Digital Texts are edited by top Shakespeare scholars. The second and more unique feature is that the Folger Digital Texts project was designed with students and web developers in mind.

Folger Digital Texts features open-source Shakespeare plays. It seems strange to use the word "open-source" in the same sentence as "Shakespeare." After all, William Shakespeare was born around 420 years before the Internet was invented. Yet it's likely that Shakespeare would be blown away by the possibilities that open-source texts provide. The Folger Digital Texts website offers PDF and XML versions of every single Shakespeare play, his sonnets, and three other poems including *Venus and Adonis* and *The Rape of Lucrece*. Folger Digital Texts encourages app developers to download the XML versions of Shakespeare plays for any noncommercial use. Developers can create games and quizzes using accurate text. And the PDF versions mean you can read Shakespeare anywhere, even if you don't have an Internet connection.

The site also makes Shakespeare's work searchable. You have the option of searching within one play or searching the whole body of work. Users can therefore search quotations, keywords, or

The Folger Shakespeare Library is located in Washington, DC.

character names. Are you wondering how many times characters use the phrase "pound of flesh" in *The Merchant of Venice*? Now it takes seconds to find out. However, the most thought-provoking aspect of the project is that texts include detailed notations. These notations reveal places where editors had to make decisions about the text after comparing several different versions of Shakespeare's plays, reminding us that Shakespeare's work has appeared in many forms over time.

List of Characters

- Antonio, the merchant
- Bassanio, Antonio's best friend; in love with Portia
- Portia, lady of Belmont; in love with Bassanio
- Shylock, Jewish moneylender
- Jessica, Shylock's daughter; in love with Lorenzo
- Gratiano, a friend of Salerio, Antonio, and Lorenzo; in love with Nerissa
- Lorenzo, friend of Gratianio; in love with Jessica
- Salerio, friend of Bassanio and Antonio
- Solanio, friend of Bassanio and Antonio; often serves as a go-between and messenger with Salerio
- The duke of Venice, judge in the courtroom
- The prince of Morocco, first suitor of Portia
- The prince of Arragon, second suitor of Portia
- Tubal, a Jewish person and friend to Shylock
- Nerissa, Portia's lady-in-waiting
- Balthazar, Portia's servant
- Launcelot Gobbo, servant to Shylock; later Bassanio's servant
- Old Gobbo, Launcelot Gobbo's father

Analysis of Major Characters

Bassanio

Is he a lazy wastrel or a respectable aristocrat? The play begins with him already in debt to Antonio and yet taking on another loan. Apparently, it was quite common in those days for aristocrats to be deeply in debt. When Nerissa and

Portia first discuss him, Bassanio is described in admirable terms: "A Venetian, (a scholar and a soldier) … in company of the Marquis of Montferrat." Not only does he possess his own strong qualities, but he also keeps good company, which this society clearly values (as does ours). Antonio, his close friend, is often praised as being a worthy gentleman.

Bassanio is the lucky recipient of the two strongest loves in the story: from Antonio and Portia. We do not see a lot of what he does or why he deserves this, and this ambiguity adds to Shakespeare's themes about money and appearance versus reality. Do we judge people too much based on what they have, how they appear, and who they spend time with? Bassanio also represents the importance of love and friendship. Antonio seems to gain his sense of purpose and source of greatness from the sacrifice he is willing to make for Bassanio. Portia is rescued from the tedious and frightening casket game by the one she really does love, Bassanio. Perhaps his strength or merit is in seeing past surfaces and recognizing the true friend and the true lover. He chooses to trust Antonio and he chooses the lead casket, the least flashy, the one with the inscription asking him to give of himself, not congratulating him for what he is or what he deserves.

Even this is not simple, however. Shakespeare never makes it easy, because life is not easy. When Bassanio chooses that lead casket, he appears virtuous, and yet the inscription is highly ironic. "Who chooseth me must give and hazard all he hath," but what has Bassanio given up thus far? He has taken, not given, a loan from Antonio that puts his dear friend's life at risk, and he has used this money to woo Portia, who gives him all of herself and her incredible wealth as soon as he passes the test.

In the trial scene, Bassanio chooses Antonio over Portia, when he says he would choose Antonio's life over hers. This is, of course, in the heat of the moment when it appears that Antonio might be losing his life. Portia pushes the point further when, disguised as the lawyer, she cajoles Bassanio into handing over the wedding ring she had given him. In this sense, Bassanio does not seem worthy of Portia's love. All sorts of references to disloyalty and instability in relationships run throughout the play, especially toward the end, yet we are still given the happy ending. After teasing their husbands and giving them quite a scare, Portia and Nerissa make up with them. Perhaps, then, Bassanio represents both the challenge and value of loving relationships.

Portia

This lovely, virtuous woman lives in posh Belmont, with old, secure money. She is desirable to all suitors, and Belmont is the place to be, free of the commercial chaos found in Venice. Like Antonio, she is in a position where she can afford to be generous to friends, even helping Antonio, who is her lover's friend. Portia remains loyal to her father by carrying out his decree with the three caskets, but she does so grudgingly. She does not seem to trust fate or her father entirely, yet her compliance is rewarded when Bassanio, her first choice, wins the prize: Portia herself.

In one sense, Portia is passive, almost symbolic. She represents mercy, heaven, and "Christian virtues." She waits in Belmont for suitors to arrive. She likes Bassanio, but must sit patiently through each visitor's attempts at the casket, and submit to whomever wins. Belmont is the paradise where, once you get there, everything seems to work itself out, as happens at the end.

Yet women are never merely submissive or subdued for Shakespeare. When Bassanio is put to the casket test, Portia sings that little song with the rhymes, perhaps as background confirmation of Bassanio's cleverness and virtue, or perhaps offering him a little sneaky clue. She can be admired for her ability to use language and disguise not only to win the day for the heroes, but also to challenge the restrictive roles of women. As a male lawyer, she displays great cleverness as she redefines the terms of the bond. She also plays with language and toys with her new husband in the ploy with the ring. The ring is typically given by the man, the terms set by him, but in this play, it is the women who do so.

Does Portia go too far with her cleverness, though? She is an actress, and she seems more excited about her disguise than about actually saving Antonio. She draws out the tension in the trial scene like a master dramatist, waiting until Shylock's knife is poised and Antonio is sure of his own death before pulling out the interpretation of the bond that will save Antonio's life. She also does this in the last act, yet the tone is light, as she and Nerissa lead their husbands quite far in their fears of their wives' infidelity, before finally sharing the trick. To be fair to Portia, however, she does the best she can in an unfair, uncomfortable world, where lovers cannot be trusted and women's lives are limited. Even in the trial scene, she may be enjoying the show to a degree, but maybe she is also making it up as she goes along, and only at the last minute is she able to figure out how to save Antonio. She is not a lawyer by training, after all. She has money, yes, but otherwise, she has more restrictions than freedom, and yet she manages

Antonio, shown here in red with Shylock, is the merchant the play is named after.

to build a life for herself that she can be happy with, and she makes all those around her happy, too.

Antonio

The play is named after this character, and yet he remains quite vague. He is wealthy and respectable, courageous and generous in offering the dangerous bond for his friend, and then coming so close to losing his life over it; yet he also keeps the religious strife and animosity with Shylock going. In the first scene where they meet, he states that friendship is impossible. Shylock mentions Antonio spitting on him and otherwise shunning him over the years. Then, in the trial scene, Antonio says it is useless trying to reason with Shylock, with his hard, Jewish heart.

Interestingly, this play's title early on was posted as either *The Merchant of Venice* or *The Jew of Venice*, a clue about this parallel between the two main characters. Notice, too, Portia's line during the trial scene: "Which is the merchant here and which the Jew?" The simple meaning, of course, is just that as a lawyer, she wants to identify the defendant and the plaintiff, but the other meaning does indicate that these two are, on some level, interchangeable. Each talks of the other as an animal. Neither can back down from hateful language and behavior, even when others are willing to make amends. Both make money from money.

Perhaps Antonio is the quintessential gambler and is uneasy at the beginning of the play because he has nothing to lose. He is a self-made man who is too successful. When Shylock offers him the crazy bond, he finally has a challenge to spark his interest. Even knowing that he may lose Bassanio or his own life, Antonio agrees.

Shylock

This character steals the show, even though he is only present in five of the play's twenty scenes. He is a fascinating, powerful, complex, and highly controversial figure. His name has become a cliché, and many who have never read the play know the name. At this level, the associations are not positive. The mythology of the greedy usurious Jew preceded *The Merchant of Venice*, but ironically, because of the realism and power of this character, the myth was kept alive by and associated with Shylock's name.

Shylock does love his money, but for him, wealth does not come or stay easily. Because of prejudices and the social and legal limitations to his success, he does not have the luxury of being generous to debtors. Since money is his only source of power and respect, he must hold onto it at all costs. He is described throughout the play as greedy and vengeful. He is equated with the devil. Clearly Christianity is the favored faith, and the "happy ending" confirms this, with Jessica choosing it and Shylock being forced into it. His Christian enemies, however, are perhaps equally corrupt, maybe even more trivial and vapid than he, for the loss of his daughter offers strong motivation for his vengeance, while they are given no such motivation. He does turn down money, too, in the trial scene. When he is offered twice the amount of the original loan, he refuses it and demands the bond. Although this vengeance seems unnecessarily brutal, he still gains sympathy. Everyone is against him in the trial scene. At the end of this scene, when Shylock says simply and quietly that he is not well, he becomes a sad, not a hateful, character. He could have stalked off angrily, or given in cheerfully, marking his conversion to Christianity as the happy ending it may appear to be. But he is pained instead, bringing out the bullying tone of the Christians surrounding him, from Portia and her merciless refusal to back down from the most extreme punishment, to the jeering crowd and Antonio's gang.

Chapter Three

A Closer Look

Themes

The Testing of Loyalty

The ring story is a source of humor and playfulness, but it also brings out one of the play's themes: how loyalty is defined and tested. Portia and Nerissa approve their husbands with the rings they offer, elicit promises about them, and then, in their alter egos of lawyer and lawyer's clerk, pressure the husbands into breaking these promises. They go so far as to claim infidelity later on. Portia announces that she invited the lawyer to her bed, which is true, of course, because she is the lawyer. Nerissa does the same.

While the husbands fail the test and the wives toy with them to an extreme degree, all is forgiven and laughed off. The more serious betrayal over a ring is when Jessica makes a mockery of the ring she took from her father, a gift from his deceased wife. Jessica ends up swapping it for a monkey while she is on her escapades with Lorenzo, and Shylock hears word of this. In a sense, loyalty and promises are taken lightly among the Christians, but they weigh heavily in the Jewish family.

Still, there is the loyalty between Antonio and Bassanio, which is very intense indeed. In the same packed scene where Portia plays the lawyer and the loyalty over the rings is tested, Bassanio asserts that his own life and his love for his wife are not worth the life of Antonio. Of course, this is a highly charged moment, when Antonio seems on the verge of losing his life, but it nonetheless points out the very strong bond between these two men.

The Effects of Money

Another theme looks at how money affects our judgment of and interactions with others. Money is central to *The Merchant of Venice*. Bassanio doesn't have enough. He has to borrow some in order to feel worthy of Portia, and he uses it to woo her. Portia is equated with monetary value when her suitors need to choose a gold, silver, or lead casket in order to win her. Is people's worth measured by their wealth?

In *Merchant*, greed is a source of pain and disappointment. This clearly involves more than just the character of Shylock. According to some readers, he actually is most sympathetic, because his own daughter betrays him. In the trial scene, when Shylock is offered three times the amount of money due him, he declines, demonstrating that he values more than money.

In a way, money fuels the whole play, which is a circle of exchanges. The same amount that Bassanio borrows from Antonio, thus binding Antonio to Shylock, is what Bassanio

The caskets demonstrate that "all that glitters is not gold."

uses to woo Portia, and once he wins her, she is the one who comes to the rescue and severs the connection between Antonio and Shylock. Shylock tries to claim ownership of Antonio's flesh, parallel to the way his Christian neighbors own slaves. The marriage bond also represents ownership.

Appearance Versus Reality

The central, unifying theme is appearance versus reality. You find this with the casket story, as a component of the money theme, and even in the inner conflicts of Shakespeare's characters. The surfaces of the caskets do not indicate what is inside, and it takes wisdom to see past the shining gold, sleek silver, and dull lead. Money can be misleading, too. Having it makes one alluring and appealing, like Portia, and yet it isn't the money that brings these characters—or us—happiness. Antonio is most happy when he gives his money away. Shylock's attachment to his money makes him miserable, and Portia falls in love with a man who is in debt. There is also a contrast or conflict between the conscious and subconscious.

Motifs

Racism

Racial conflict is a motif that pushes the dramatic tension and heightens the play's themes. Perhaps Shakespeare understood quite well the perspective of a member of an oppressed group. If Antonio or Bassanio misbehaved, they would be criticized as individuals, but if Shylock missteps, he is judged as the representative of his entire race. If this is so in this play, then Shylock's vengeance too is for all Jews. "Thou call'dst me dog before thou hadst a cause, / But since I am a dog, beware my fangs." Perhaps Shylock's only source of power and respect is through money, which is why he hates Antonio for lending it free of interest; Antonio, given his social status, can afford to be generous.

The endless cycle of generalizing or stereotyping is set in motion, so Shylock comments during the trial scene that he would hate the idea of his daughter marrying such "Christian husbands" as Antonio and Bassanio, who claim their friendship to be greater than their bonds

With his daughter choosing to leave his house and having been denied his vengeance, there is no happy ending for Shylock (Roger Wreford).

with their wives. And then, of course, the "happy ending" has Shylock forced to convert to Christianity, as Jessica has done, and will all of his fortune to her and her new Christian husband. To the Venetians, "Christian" is good and "Jewish" is bad, but the play's tensions and ambiguities question this, showing the pain and loss associated with such hateful generalizations. It is not completely clear how much the generalizations are included simply to please Shakespeare's audience by reflecting prejudices, and how much he is presenting a situation for analysis and critique of his society's flawed thinking (and ours).

Setting

Setting serves as a motif, bringing out themes quite starkly in this play, with Venice representing the uneasiness, chaos,

AFTER THE TRIAL: ANTONIO RECEIVING THE CONGRATULATIONS OF HIS FRIENDS.—"Merchant of Venice."
BY HENRY WALLIS.

Antonio celebrates being released from his bond.

Modern Stagings

OVER TIME, CREATIVE directors of theater companies have experimented with innovative ways of staging Shakespeare's classic plays. One theater company has made their mark catering to audiences with short attention spans and a healthy sense of humor. The Reduced Shakespeare Company was founded in 1981 by three actors who call themselves "the bad boys of abridgment." The Reduced Shakespeare Company has since branched out beyond the work of the Bard, but they made a name for themselves staging *The Complete Works of William Shakespeare (abridged)*. The play condenses thirty-seven of Shakespeare's plays into one ninety-minute comedy show. The three actors wear historical garb (including tights), along with Converse sneakers as they sprint through the main points of Shakespeare's plays. The Reduced Shakespeare Company continues to tour the world performing *The Complete Works of William Shakespeare (abridged)* today.

But The Reduced Shakespeare Company isn't the only theater company putting their own spin on Shakespeare plays. It's not unusual to hear about a production set in modern day, a play told through modern dance, or performances by all-female casts. In early 2015, director Rupert Goold reimagined *The Merchant of Venice*. His version was set in present-day Las Vegas. In Goold's retelling, the contest for Portia's hand in marriage takes place on a reality show.

Jess Borgeson, Daniel Singer, and Adam Lang of the Reduced Shakespeare Company pose with a fan.

And now you can direct your own version of a scene from *Macbeth*, *A Midsummer Night's Dream*, or *Much Ado about Nothing*, thanks to an interactive activity called "Staging It" on the Globe Theater's website. "Staging It" lets you select from four performances of each line in the scene to make your own short film. The activity is a hands-on way to understand how a director shapes our understanding of a play and how the staging of a play can help us connect to the work.

and brutality of commerce and capitalism, while peaceful Belmont is the placid site of old money and values. Venice is a man's world. Even when Portia and Nerissa visit, they are disguised as men; the objects found there are money bags and Shylock's knife, while Belmont is a woman's world, with men coming only as wooers and suitors. The props associated with this moonlit location are connected with women and fairy tales: rings, caskets, and music. Belmont is where everyone wants to go, and only the "villain," Shylock, does not make it there. Antonio, his nemesis, goes there briefly, and yet remains aloof and unattached.

As with everything else for Shakespeare, the distinctions between these two settings and what they represent are not clear-cut. Jessica seems not fully welcome in blissful Belmont. Portia is not fully kind or merciful in the trial scene, and of course Shylock is not fully bad or Antonio fully good. Money itself and its powers are not completely dirty or negative. Venice comes to Belmont and Belmont to Venice. We are never separate from our basest instincts or our heavenly goodness.

Symbols

Wedding Rings

The wedding rings represent wedding vows (and Bassanio says he would cut off his left hand defending the ring) and the female body. As stated above, money is, in a way, the hero that fixes everything, at least on a superficial level (but its allures and surface appeal are dangerous, too). Another way of looking at it is that money itself is not good or bad. How people use it and give it value determines its goodness or evil.

Language

Literary critic Norman N. Holland looks closely at how different the two settings, Venice and Belmont, are, even in terms of the language used in each. As has already been pointed out, Venice represents harsh, determined commercialism, while Belmont represents a fairy-tale paradise. In Venice, the characters talk about money and

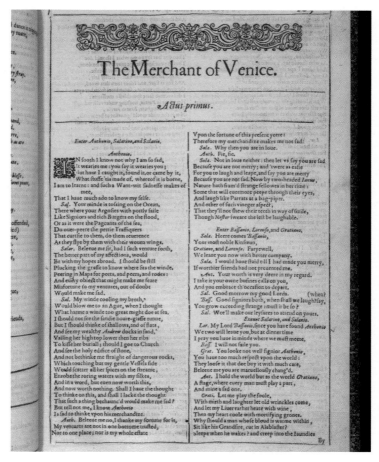

The language used in the play develops the contrast between Venice and Belmont.

investments, while in Belmont, they refer to mythology and fairy tales. In Belmont, all is love, harmony and music. Lorenzo and Jessica share their loving exchanges, referring to legendary lovers such as Troilus and Cressida and Pyramus and Thisbe. They also talk of the calming, celebratory effects of music. This contrasts with Shylock back in Venice, who has no interest in the masque and warns Jessica to close the windows against the noise.

In Venice, there is worry and scarcity. Solanio and Salerio talk of the merchant's worried frame of mind: "… every object that might make me fear / Misfortune to my ventures, out of doubt / Would make me sad." While in Belmont, there is excess and growth: "… yet for you / I would be trebled twenty times myself, / A thousand times more fair, ten thousand times more rich …" Portia brings this world of plenty to Venice when she enters the courtroom and asks that Shylock give mercy: "It is twice blest; / It blesseth him that gives and him that takes."

The use of assonance and internal rhyme in this play is highly successful, from the opening speeches of the first act to some of the more famous speeches, such as Portia's speech on mercy. Shylock, on the other hand, is associated with prose. He moves the drama forward, forcing characters to respond to him, not the audience. This play can be studied in terms of Shakespeare's developing skills. In earlier plays, prose serves the plot and poetry is a divergence, often offering the playwright direct input on important themes. Later in this play, however, poetic language is also used in taut, plot-pushing moments, such as when a servant announces Bassanio's arrival to Belmont in

Shakespeare blends poetry and prose in his plays.

sonnetlike language. "A day in April never came so sweet, / To show how costly summer was at hand …" Act III, Scene 1 shows the first time a major character (Shylock) speaks only serious, dramatic prose. This mixed use of prose and verse is considered more sophisticated than what is found in Shakespeare's earlier plays, and leads toward the plays that follow.

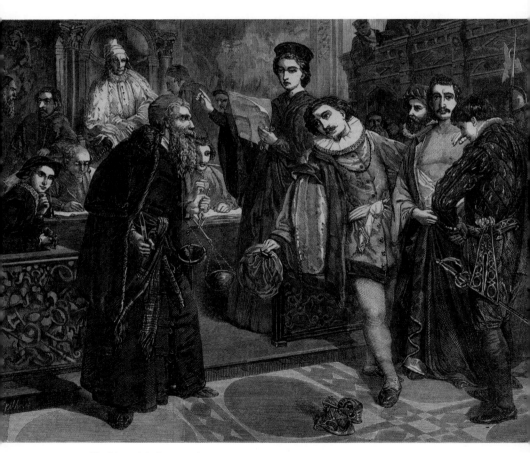

All of Antonio's lines are in verse.

Still Shakespeare does not give language obvious value or status. The theme of appearance versus reality (or lead versus gold) applies to language as well. Characters often mock themselves or others for talking too much and speaking empty words, or comment that wisdom is often hidden in silence, masked by words. Another Shakespeare scholar, G. R. Hibbard, notes that while prose and verse mark the lowest to the highest status in characters, from Launcelot Gobbo on the one end of the continuum to the duke on the other, at the same time, with the Shylock–Antonio opposition or the money versus love conflict, there aren't clear or obvious distinctions. Instead he observes that the whole play is about trials: Antonio's friendship with Bassanio is tried or tested; Bassanio's love for Portia is on trial with the trick of the rings; there is the literal trial, of course, with Shylock and Antonio; and Portia's loyalty to her father is tested by means of the casket riddles. In both prose and verse, the mode of communication is argumentative. Logic is used to justify choices. Launcelot's speech mocks this in Act II, Scene 2, when he says that while we refer to logic, it is actually pleasure and convenience that dictate our decisions.

Antonio is the only character who speaks entirely in verse. He also shares his feelings directly, which puts him in a vulnerable position. The only time when he uses this language of argument is in his very hateful speech during the trial, when he compares Shylock to uncontrollable features of nature, saying that he would be as impossible to change as these. Antonio and Shylock are opponents and opposites. Shylock's language is guarded and careful, even though his emotions are clearly just as powerful as Antonio's. Shylock uses repetition and calculation.

The pattern of building up an argument and using repetition, like that of a debater or politician, comes forth passionately and dramatically in Shylock's "Hath not a Jew eyes" speech. Shylock, though, is ever practical, and his speech moves away from figurative into the literal, for example, "land-rats and water-rats, water-thieves and land thieves … I mean pirates" or "stop my house's ears—I mean my casements." Shylock's calculating, cautious style puts him in a powerful position. Yet Shylock's strength and coolness are turned against him in mockery when he loses the trial and slinks from the room, utterly defeated. Still his power is felt. As the character with perhaps the most dramatic and effective speeches, once he is gone from the play, the conversation of love, jokes about the rings, and other discussions appear as trivial chatter. The weight of Shylock and what he represents is not lost. In the spirit of a romantic comedy, the play closes in Belmont, with all sorts of happy resolutions, and yet there are references to infidelity, and the character who has the last word, Gratiano, is not a particularly appealing one. Shakespeare never glosses over truths. The arguments are not finished.

Interpreting the Play

The Merchant of Venice is a messy play in that it combines three found stories, seems to be neither a comedy nor a tragedy, and presents controversial topics in highly ambiguous ways. Some critics find it imperfect for these reasons, an experiment that did not quite succeed. Just because Shakespeare is very famous and brilliant, there is no reason not to find flaws in his work.

Literary critics can evaluate *The Merchant of Venice* from many perspectives, including through a feminist lens.

Literary criticism of the work seems to follow two main trends: one that looks at it in terms of fairy tale and allegory, and the other that looks at the realism of it through the lens of feminist or other modern theories. According to Craig Bernthal, those who miss the allegorical element are unwilling to accept the play in its historical context, and force modern interpretations on it that are not appropriate, including labeling it as sexist, anti-Semitic, or heterosexist.

Perhaps this need not be an either/or option. Following the first approach, one would appreciate the pound of flesh story as allegorical and not to be taken literally. (And, in one sense, Shylock fails when he tries to force the merry bond into a literal interpretation.) Portia and her caskets represent an old tale of the princess and the three princes—always three—and always the third wins. This same princess story (also in *King Lear*, the story of the judgment of Paris, and *Cinderella*) is interpreted along these lines as representing man's movement toward death. The princess in her youth and beauty actually represents the opposite: death, but also "Mother Earth," to whom we all return.

In a religious interpretation, Belmont ("beautiful mountain") represents heaven, where those who sacrifice are rewarded. The plot represents an allegorical journey toward spiritual life or death. Commercial, corrupt Venice threatens the spiritual life, but those who can eschew dirty money obsessions gain access to Belmont, heaven, the spiritual life. (Of course, ironically, Portia has no need to worry about money or trouble herself with the business of acquiring wealth.) Portia says she "stands for sacrifice." Bassanio chooses the casket with the inscription that mentions giving, not receiving. Jessica runs away from her moneylending father. Lorenzo exclaims, "Fair ladies, you drop manna in the way / Of starved people," referring to heavenly communion. All who enter Belmont have left Venice both physically and symbolically.

What confuses audiences and readers is that the play is not a fairy tale. There is a gritty realism and a lack of the whimsical, magical elements that you might find in some of Shakespeare's other comedies. Shylock is not clearly, simply bad, nor are Antonio and his friends clearly, simply good. The relationships that do work out are unsteady, with Bassanio and Gratiano breaking the promise of the rings, Bassanio choosing Antonio over Portia in the trial scene, and Jessica being applauded for converting to Christianity, though she is still somehow an outsider in Belmont. Part of truly appreciating Shakespeare and what he is saying about life, is holding opposing views and feelings at once, accepting conflicting theories about the play, accepting conflicting tones to it, and embracing the ambiguities within characters and their relationships.

CHRONOLOGY

1564 William Shakespeare is born on April 23 in Stratford-upon-Avon, England

1578–1582 Span of Shakespeare's "Lost Years," covering the time between leaving school and marrying Anne Hathaway of Stratford

1582 At age eighteen, Shakespeare marries Anne Hathaway, age twenty-six, on November 28

1583 Susanna Shakespeare, William and Anne's first child, is born in May, six months after the wedding

1584 Birth of twins Hamnet and Judith Shakespeare

1585–1592 Shakespeare leaves his family in Stratford to become an actor and playwright in a London theater company

1587 Public beheading of Mary Queen of Scots

1593–1594 The Bubonic (Black) Plague closes theaters in London

1594–1596 As a leading playwright, Shakespeare creates some of his most popular works, including *A Midsummer Night's Dream* and *Romeo and Juliet*

1596 Hamnet Shakespeare dies in August at age eleven, possibly of plague

1596–1597 *The Merchant of Venice* and *Henry IV, Part One* are most likely written

1599 The Globe Theatre opens

1600 *Julius Caesar* is first performed at the Globe

1600–1601 *Hamlet* is believed to have been written

1601–1602 *Twelfth Night* is probably composed

1603 Queen Elizabeth dies; Scottish king James VI succeeds her and becomes England's James I

1604 Shakespeare pens *Othello*

1605 *Macbeth* is composed

1608–1610 London's theaters are forced to close when the plague returns and kills an estimated thirty-three thousand people

1611 *The Tempest* is written

1613 The Globe Theatre is destroyed by fire

1614 The reopening of the Globe

1616 Shakespeare dies on April 23

1623 Anne Hathaway, Shakespeare's widow, dies; a collection of Shakespeare's plays, known as the First Folio, is published

A SHAKESPEARE GLOSSARY

addition A name or title, such as knight, duke, duchess, king, etc.

affect To like or love; to be attracted to.

approve To prove or confirm.

attend To pay attention.

belike Probably.

beseech To beg or request.

bondman A slave.

bootless Futile; useless; in vain.

broil A battle.

charge Expense, responsibility; to command or accuse.

common A term describing the common people, below nobility.

condition Social rank; quality.

countenance Face; appearance; favor.

cousin A relative.

curious Careful; attentive to detail.

discourse To converse; conversation.

discover To reveal or uncover.

dispatch To speed or hurry; to send; to kill.

doubt To suspect.

entreat To beg or appeal.

envy To hate or resent; hatred; resentment.

ere Before.

eyne Eyes.

fain Gladly.

fare To eat; to prosper.

favor Face, privilege.

fellow A peer or equal.

filial Of a child toward its parent.

fine An end; "in fine" means in sum.

folio A book made up of individually printed sheets, each
folded in half to make four pages. Shakespeare's folios contain
all of his known plays in addition to other works.

fond Foolish.

fool A darling.

genius A good or evil spirit.

gentle Well-bred; not common.

gentleman One whose labor was done by servants. (Note:
to call someone a *gentleman* was not a mere compliment on his
manners; it meant that he was above the common people.)

gentles People of quality.

get To beget (a child).

go to "Go on"; "come off it."

go we Let us go.

haply Perhaps.

happily By chance; fortunately.

hard by Nearby.

heavy Sad or serious.

husbandry Thrift; economy.

instant Immediate.

kind One's nature; species.

knave A villain; a poor man.

lady A woman of high social rank. (Note: *lady* was not a synonym for *woman* or *polite woman*; it was not a compliment but simply a word referring to one's actual legal status in society, like *gentleman*.)

leave Permission; "take my leave" means depart (with permission).

lief, lieve "I had as lief" means I would just as soon; I would rather.

like To please; "it likes me not" means it is disagreeable to me.

livery The uniform of a nobleman's servants; emblem.

Lord Chamberlain's Men The company of players Shakespeare joined in London; under James I they became the King's Men.

mark Notice; pay attention.

morrow Morning.

needs Necessarily.

nice Too fussy or fastidious.

owe To own.

passing Very.

peculiar Individual; exclusive.

privy Private; secret.

proper Handsome; one's very own ("his proper son").

protest To insist or declare.

quite Completely.

require Request.

several Different, various.

severally Separately.

sirrah A term used to address social inferiors.

sooth Truth.

state Condition; social rank.

still Always; persistently.

success Result(s).

surfeit Fullness.

touching Concerning; about; as for.

translate To transform.

unfold To disclose.

verse Writing that uses a regular metrical rhythm and is divided from other lines by a space.

villain A low or evil person; originally, a peasant.

voice A vote; consent; approval.

vouchsafe To confide or grant.

vulgar Common.

want To lack.

weeds Clothing.

what ho "Hello, there!"

wherefore Why.

wit Intelligence; sanity.

withal Moreover; nevertheless.

without Outside.

would Wish.

SUGGESTED ESSAY TOPICS

1. Does money bring you happiness? Look at how the major characters in *The Merchant of Venice* use and value money. What is Shakespeare telling us about how it affects us or how we should think about it?

2. Do the female characters in *The Merchant of Venice* run the show? Are they secretly the real movers and shakers, and do they have to disguise their intelligence and abilities because they are in subservient positions?

3. Watch two film versions of the same scene. Comment on the decisions the directors made to bring out a particular theme (see above for possible themes or motifs on which to focus). Which touches do you like best? Is there anything you would do differently if you were making this film? Make sure to focus on the one theme or motif that you selected.

4. Can we judge people by those with whom they spend time? Look at Antonio and his group of friends, or other groupings, such as Portia and Nerissa, or characters who choose to leave one affiliation for another (Jessica leaves Shylock for Lorenzo; Launcelot leaves Shylock for Bassanio; Bassanio chooses Portia, and in a way, leaves Antonio). What does this tell us about the person? Is it fair to judge people this way?

5. True spirituality is rare. Hypocrisy prevails. Is this true in *The Merchant of Venice*? Are there any characters who adhere to their religions in a respectable and respectful manner?

TEST YOUR MEMORY

1. Which character is "the merchant" of the title?
  a) Shylock; b) Bassanio; c) Launcelot; d) Antonio.

2. Which casket does the prince of Morocco choose?
  a) gold; b) silver; c) lead; d) none; Portia sends him away early.

3. How much money does Shylock lend in the bond
  with Antonio?
  a) 500 ducats; b) 1,000 ducats; c) 3,000 ducats; d) 6,000
  ducats.

4. Shylock asks that Jessica respond to the masque in which way?
  a) Shut all doors and windows and ignore the music and noise;
  b) Join in the fun, but be careful; c) Enjoy the music, but don't
  go outside; d) Accompany him to the party.

5. What does the prince of Arragon get from his choice
  of caskets?
  a) a flower; b) nothing; c) a picture of Portia; d) a fool's head.

6. Which character says, in a famous speech, "If you prick us, do
  we not bleed? If you tickle us, do we not laugh? If you poison
  us, do we not die? And if you wrong us, shall we not revenge?"
  a) Antonio; b) the duke; c) Bassanio; d) Shylock.

7. Jessica traded the ring from her mother for what?
  a) a dress; b) wine and lodging; c) a monkey;
  d) passage on a ship.

8. What news does Bassanio receive just after winning Portia's hand?
a) Antonio cannot repay Shylock; b) Antonio will come visit him in Belmont; c) Launcelot would like to be his servant; d) Jessica has run away with Lorenzo.

9. Where does Portia say she and Nerissa will wait for their new husbands while they take care of the business with Shylock and Antonio?
a) at home in Belmont; b) in a nearby country home; c) in Venice; d) at a monastery.

10. When Shylock is asked to back down from his pursuit of the bond, his response is:
a) I will if you pay me three times the original amount; b) You could pay me more than six times the amount, and I still wouldn't back down; c) If only Antonio would apologize, I'd end this; d) Bring back my daughter, and then we can talk.

11. Which character says this in a famous speech? "The quality of mercy is not strained, / It droppeth as the gentle rain from heaven / Upon the place beneath."
a) Portia; b) Antonio; c) the duke; d) Shylock.

12. What trick does Portia as the lawyer use to turn the trial around?
a) Shylock can't use a knife; b) Shylock must accept twice the original loan instead; c) Shylock may cut, but cannot let Antonio bleed; d) Since Shylock is not a Christian, he has to wait before the bond can be recognized.

13. In what way does Antonio "compromise" with Shylock at the end of the trial?
a) He requires that Shylock pay back all interest charged to others, in return for his life; b) He requires that Shylock convert to Christianity, and will the forfeiture due Antonio to Jessica and Lorenzo, but be allowed to live; c) He requires that Shylock leave Venice and never return, but not owe any fine; d) He says that Shylock must stop the usury business and then be free.

Answer Key

1. d; 2. a; 3. c; 4. a; 5. d; 6. d; 7. c; 8. a; 9. d; 10. b; 11. a; 12. c; 13. b

FURTHER INFORMATION

Books

Hinds, Gareth. *The Merchant of Venice (Graphic Shakespeare)*. Cambridge, MA: Candlewick Press, 2008.

Middleton, Haydn. *True Lives: Shakespeare*. New York: Oxford University Press, 2009.

Mittelstaedt, Walt. *Understanding Literature: A Student's Guide to William Shakespeare*. Berkeley Heights, NJ: Enslow Publishers, 2005.

Websites

Folger Digital Texts
www.folgerdigitaltexts.org

Read and download full-text, searchable versions of Shakespeare's plays and sonnets.

In Search of Shakespeare
www.bardweb.net

The Shakespeare Resource Center includes a roundup of links to the best Shakespeare information on the Internet, organized by topic.

Staging It

www.shakespearesglobe.com/discovery-space/staging-it

Direct a Shakespeare scene through this interactive activity created by the Globe Theatre.

Films

The Merchant of Venice. Directed by Chris Hunt and Trevor Nunn, a British television production starring Henry Goodman, Alexander Hanson, and Derbhle Crotty, 2001.

The Merchant of Venice. Directed by Michael Radford, starring Al Pacino, Joseph Fiennes, and Lynn Collins, 2004.

Audiobooks and Recordings

The Merchant of Venice, Stratford Festival on CD. Narrators: Peter Hutt, Donald Carrier. Canadian Broadcasting Company, 2002.

The Merchant of Venice on CD. Narrators: Haydn Gwynne, Bill Nighy, Arkangel Cast. Published by Audio Partners, Auburn, CA, 2005.

BIBLIOGRAPHY

Bernthal, Craig. T*he Trial of Man: Christianity and Judgment in the World of Shakespeare*. Wilmington, DE: ISI Books, 2003.

Calderwood, James L. and Harold E. Toliver, eds. *Essays in Shakespearean Criticism*. Englewood Cliffs, NJ: Prentice-Hall Inc., 1970.

Epstein, Norrie. *The Friendly Shakespeare: A Thoroughly Painless Guide to the Best of the Bard*. New York: Viking, A Winokur/Boates Book, 1993.

Goddard, Harold C. *The Meaning of Shakespeare, Vol. 1*. 81–116. Chicago: The University of Chicago Press, 1967.

Goddard, Harold C. "Portia Fails the Test for Inner Gold." In *Readings on "The Merchant of Venice."* Edited by Clarice Swisher. San Diego: Greenhaven Press Inc., 2000.

Gross, John. *Shylock: A Legend and Its Legacy*. New York: Simon and Schuster, 1992.

Halliday, F. E. "Poetry and Prose in *The Merchant of Venice*." In *Readings on "The Merchant of Venice."* Edited by Clarice Swisher. San Diego: Greenhaven Press Inc., 2000.

Hibbard, G. R. "The Language of Argument in *The Merchant of Venice*." In *Readings on "The Merchant of Venice."* Edited by Clarice Swisher. San Diego: Greenhaven Press Inc., 2000.

Holland, Norman M. "Two Contrasting Worlds in *The Merchant of Venice*." In *Readings on "The Merchant of Venice*." Edited by Clarice Swisher. San Diego: Greenhaven Press Inc., 2000.

Kay, Dennis. "The Historical Context of *The Merchant of Venice*." In *Readings on "The Merchant of Venice*." Edited by Clarice Swisher. San Diego: Greenhaven Press Inc., 2000.

McEvoy, Sean. *Shakespeare: The Basics*. London: Routledge, 2000.

The Merchant of Venice. Directed by Michael Radford. Sony Pictures Classics, Film Council, Film Fund Luxemburg, 2004.

Turner, Frederick. *Shakespeare's Twenty-First Century Economics: The Morality of Love and Money*. Oxford: Oxford University Press, 1999.

Wolf, Matt. "High-Concept Shakespeare and a Dash of Hope." *The New York Times*. December 19, 2014.

INDEX

ABOUT THE AUTHOR

Caitlyn Paley lives in Maryland, where she works in classrooms and writes books for students. Paley is the author of *Strategic Inventions of the Revolutionary War*, the introduction to *King Lear* in the Reading Shakespeare Today series, and two books for middle school students—all from Cavendish Square Publishing. Paley enjoys doing research, hiking, and exploring the world. *The Merchant of Venice* is her favorite Shakespeare play.